THE
POWER
OF
PRAYER

ACCORDING
TO THE PATTERN

THE POWER OF PRAYER

ACCORDING TO THE PATTERN

By Sandy Sims & C.J. Thomas

Published by:
Sharing The Light Ministries
P.O. Box 596
Lithia Springs, GA 30122
www.myholycall.com

ISBN 0-9646515-2-1
Printed in the United States of America

**All scripture quotations are taken from
The King James Version**
(Bold, capitals, and italics added for emphasis)

Illustrations from
"The Tabernacle In the Wilderness"
Copyright © 1976, 1999 By Gerth Medien GmbH,
Asslar, Germany

Book cover design by Mark Hayes for
The Establishment Group
www.theestablishmentgroup.net

"Praying the Tabernacle Pattern is the removing of the veil which has separated the Church from the Holy of Holies for so long. I have personally had the privilege of ordaining, imparting to and speaking into the lives of Sandy and C.J. and can attest that their "Pattern" is straight from the throne! When the disciples asked Jesus to teach them to pray, this was that teaching."

Micheal Pipes
Next Move of God Ministries

Dedication

This book is dedicated to the Father, Son and Holy
Spirit. Thank You for saving our lives and blessing us
to know Your heart and Your vision for the Body of
Christ and the end-time harvest of souls.

We would also like to give special thanks to our loving
husbands, families, friends and intercessors. We love
you all and thank you for your love and support.
Daily we pray God's richest
blessings upon you.

Preface

What we are about to share with you has been hidden in the Word and the heart of God for such a time as this!

This revelation is a gift from the Father to bless and unify the Body of Christ into His mighty invincible army. This corporate anointing will manifest the presence of God. Whether you are a part of the five-fold ministry, a seasoned Saint or a new convert in Christ, this revelation will bless God; bless you, and the world. It will also propel you into the Secret Place, the very presence of God!

We are God's end-time army, hand-picked, to bring in the final harvest and to fill the earth with His glory. In order to accomplish this task, WE MUST UNITE IN PRAYER! To the natural mind that seems impossible as we look at the landscape of all the different denominations and Church doctrines. However, with God—ALL THINGS ARE POSSIBLE!

Within this book you will see how the manifold wisdom of God has overcome denominational barriers. It has also overcome the gulf between Jew and Gentile, and every other obstacle to create His *"One New Man"* (Eph 2:15). The most spectacular element is the exponential multiplication (extremely rapid increase) of prayer power for the end-time harvest. Your royal priesthood enables you to pray for and on behalf of 6½ billion people! Yes, just one king-priest has that much power! Two king-priests produce 13 billion prayers. Three king-priests produce 19½ billion prayers. One can easily see **"The Awesome Power of God"** that will be released when the Church enters her king-priest ministry. Our God is a wise God!

To our Jewish brothers and sisters, true repentance by the Church and an apology has been long overdue. Therefore we stand in the gap and repent for all the atrocities that have happened to you throughout history by the Church. In addition, we repent for the actions of all others, past and present, inspired by satan to harm you.

We would also like to thank you for preserving the Word of God, keeping the Sabbaths, and celebrating the Feasts. The preservation of your rich heritage enabled us to see the manifold wisdom of God. You are truly God's chosen people and we thank you for being the vehicle through which God brought the Messiah to earth.

To our Gentile Christian brothers and sisters, we pray that you also have this heart of repentance and deep appreciation for the Jewish people. Whether or not they have received Jesus as Messiah, they need to know what an awesome blessing they have been. These heart attitudes create the foundation God needs to pour out His glory upon the entire earth! In John 17:21-22, Jesus prayed that we would be one so the world would know God sent His Son. He also said, if we became one the same glory upon Jesus would be upon us. This is the end-time glory everyone is waiting for—**THE AWESOME POWER OF GOD!**

Much Love, Blessings & Shalom!
Sandy Sims & C.J. Thomas

The Power of Prayer
According To The Pattern

Contents

The Tabernacle
Of Moses

The High Priest Of Israel

Foreword

This book provides revelation on the most important aspect of Christianity, which is prayer. The teaching by Jesus in Matthew 6:9-13, the Lord's Prayer, is a model or pattern for prayer. Revelation 1:5-6 states that by the Blood of Jesus we have been made *"kings and priests"* unto God. According to I Peter 2:9, we are a *"royal priesthood"* to show forth the praises of our God. Within the Tabernacle of Moses there are shadow pictures that show a relationship between the model prayer and our royal priesthood.

Understanding the true meaning and the correlation between the Lord's model prayer, the Tabernacle and our royal priesthood will bring in the glory of God and His end-time harvest of souls!

The main reason why we have not fulfilled this holy calling is because we have not understood our adoption. We have been adopted into Jesus' family. Jesus was born Jewish, in Israel, and we have been adopted into the Lord's family. Yet unfortunately we know little or nothing about this beautiful heritage we have been given.

Our Jewish family has a way of worship that will manifest the presence of God. God Himself, thousands of years ago, established this way of worship. However, we have not entered into that way of worship or taken the time to learn about it. In this book you will learn how to pray and worship God according to His divine will.

This book simply introduces your holy calling to be a king-priest unto God and provides a step-by-step method for fulfilling it. It also provides tips on praying the Pattern and a template for you to create your own Prayer Pattern. For more in-depth information and scriptures regarding your royal priesthood and how to pray according to the Pattern please see the parent book **"The Awesome Power Of God – Praying According To The Pattern"**.

However, for those who want to *"just do it"*, let's begin by asking God right now to remove the veil from our hearts and minds. Then we will be able to understand the powerful truths He has hidden within the Tabernacle of Moses.

The Writings Of Moses

Jesus expressed just how important the writings of Moses are in this scripture.

John 5:46-47
For had ye believed Moses, ye would have believed me: for he wrote of me. But if ye believe not his writings, how shall ye believe my words?

Jesus was saying; if we don't believe what Moses wrote about Him, how can we believe what He has to say? How did Moses write about Jesus? Moses wrote the first five books of the Bible, part of which he details the building of the Tabernacle and how to worship therein! The Tabernacle tells of the accomplishments, attributes, characteristics and the glory of God in Jesus Christ.

The Tabernacle of Moses is one of the most spectacular creations that God has given to mankind. Just to give you a brief description of how important it is, let's examine the scriptures. Exodus 25:8 states that God told Moses to build Him a Tabernacle so that He could come and dwell with them. The Tabernacle made it possible for the holiness of God to dwell with man upon the earth. Hebrews 8:2 tells us that the Tabernacle of Moses is a replica of the true Tabernacle in heaven and that Jesus is the High Priest and Minister of that Tabernacle. The Tabernacle is a shadow picture of the life, death, resurrection, and total dominion of Jesus Christ. Every detail of the Tabernacle testifies of Jesus Christ, the Lamb of God!

Revelation 1:5-6 and 5:9-10 tell us that by the Blood of Jesus, we have been made kings and priests unto God. First Peter 2:9 states that we are a royal priesthood, a holy nation to show forth God's praises. Jesus is our great King and High Priest ministering in the heavenly Tabernacle. And He has made us king-priests; therefore we should learn how to fulfill this ministry. This book provides everything we need to understand this holy calling and to FULFILL IT.

The essence of this calling is to pray the Word of God according to the Pattern of the Tabernacle. As you begin to pray according to Pattern you will see your life change in a marvelous way. In Matthew 6:9-13, Jesus was giving instructions on how to pray. He said; **"AFTER THIS MANNER THEREFORE PRAY"**. Jesus was giving us a model or pattern for prayer. This means that we should follow the points brought out in the pattern. Prayer, *"AFTER THIS MANNER"*, is in the exact Pattern of the Tabernacle of Moses! We have also included the correlation of each section to the Lord's Prayer (Matthew 6:9-13) within the Tabernacle Prayer Pattern.

Uniting The World In Prayer

John 17:21
That they all may be one; as thou, Father, art in me, and I in thee, that they also may be one in us: that the world may believe that thou hast sent me.

When Jesus made this statement He was talking about the Jews and Gentiles coming together as one. At that time there were no Christian denominations, just JEWS AND GENTILES. Jesus said that this unity would cause the world to know that God sent His Son!

The Jews were given the divine order of worship in the Torah (Tabernacle and the Feasts). However, many do not understand that Jesus is the fulfillment of the shadow pictures. On the other hand, many Gentiles have received Christ as the Messiah, but know nothing about their Jewish heritage.

Jesus wanted the Jews to understand that He is the Messiah and the fulfillment of the Torah and worship Him in that manner. He also wanted Gentiles to take their knowledge of Him as Messiah and apply that to the divine order of worship He gave the Jews. This is the true meaning of the unity Jesus was talking about!

When we unite in this type of worship it will cause the WORLD to know that God sent His Son! Jesus said if we united the same glory that rested upon Him would be upon us! GLORY TO GOD! Praying according to Pattern will accomplish this!

Hidden in the Tabernacle of Moses is the power and ability to unite all in prayer, performing the desires of God's heart. We may all differ in doctrines but if we belong to God and honor His Word; we can all come into agreement upon what Jesus accomplished as the fulfillment of the Tabernacle. This gives us a basis for agreement whereby we can come together and worship the Lord in one accord. This will fulfill the following scripture, *"Till we all come in the unity of the faith, and of the knowledge of the Son of God, unto a perfect man, unto the measure of the stature of the fulness of Christ"* (Ephesians 4:13).

It is and always has been God's desire to bring us together as one (John 17:21). One day in prayer, I began to ponder the importance of praying according to Pattern. As the different benefits began to flow across my mind, I heard the Holy Spirit ask, "Have you ever heard of an army that was not organized?" That startled me because the Church is supposed to be the army of God but to date we have no organization! In every army there is government, unification, and specific goals and objectives. With the Tabernacle Prayer Pattern, we can become the mighty army of God. The divine order of the Tabernacle prayer displays God's government. It also brings unification and by virtue of the declared Word of God establishes God's objectives in the earth.

The Tabernacle Prayer Pattern is so unique and multi-faceted that it can be prayed in several different ways. A prayer leader can pray it alone while everyone else comes into agreement. You can also have two people alternate as we do, or you can have a group of people, with each person praying a section of the Tabernacle. Another way is to simply follow the leader, with each person adding scriptures applicable to that section. The ultimate level is our desire to bring the Church together, globally, through satellite. We would have each country pray a section of the Tabernacle so the entire Body of Christ, Jew and Gentile Christians, can come together and worship God as one. When we unify, the glory of God will manifest and the world will know that God sent His Son, the Lord Jesus Christ!

As you begin to pray this way, you will notice the growth in your spirit-man because praying this Pattern is establishing the Word of God in your life. It is essential to understand that there is no greater force in the universe than the Word of God. The angels or ministering spirits hearken unto the voice of His Word, not your opinions or ability to speak well, so ***please pray the Word of God!*** You will be empowered and learn how to bring *"true worship"* to the Father, Son, and Holy Spirit, in a powerful way.

In your hand is a book that provides everything you need to fulfill this holy calling! Let's not keep our Father waiting one minute longer, lets go forth to experience **"The Power Of Prayer – According to The Pattern!"**

The Vision Of Unity!

Your King-Priest Ministry

God, through Moses His prophet, commanded Pharaoh to let His people go so they may worship Him. Through God's mighty hand, the Israelites were delivered from slavery in Egypt. In the wilderness of Sinai, Moses was given precise instructions by God to build a Tabernacle, a place to worship and serve Him. In Exodus 25:8 the Lord said, *"And let them make me a sanctuary; that I may dwell among them"*.

The building of the Tabernacle was for the purpose of God dwelling among His people. He gave His people a way to receive atonement for their sins, and a method of approach to Him. In God's manifold wisdom He also made everything within the

Tabernacle a shadow picture prophesying the life and ministry of the Lord Jesus Christ—the Lamb of God. Glory to God, the Tabernacle not only stands as a testimony of God's plan of redemption, but also gives us the perfect way to worship Him!

Jesus Himself made a powerful statement when He said in John 14:6; I AM THE WAY, THE TRUTH AND THE LIFE AND NO MAN COMES TO THE FATHER BUT BY ME. The Jews understood that He was speaking of the pathway through the Tabernacle. The entrances to the Outer and Inner courts and the Holy of Holies were known as the WAY, the TRUTH, and the LIFE. Jesus, in essence, was saying I AM THE TABERNACLE! He was also confirming there is a divine order of prayer that must be followed in order to get into the presence of the Father.

Let's begin our study of the Prayer Pattern with the linen gate that surrounded the Tabernacle of Moses. This is where we repent and enter God's gates with thanksgiving and His courts with praise. The first piece of furniture within the Tabernacle was the Brazen Altar where the animals were sacrificed. This is symbolic of Jesus, the Lamb of God, Who took away the sins of the world on the Brazen Altar of Calvary. We praise Jesus for shedding His Blood and redeeming us.

The second piece of furniture was the Brazen Laver. It was a basin of water where the priests would wash before ministering unto the Lord. At this Laver we thank Him that He is the Word made flesh and that we are washed by the water of His Word.

The next piece of furniture was the Candlestick or Lampstand. It is symbolic of Jesus, the Light of the world, anointed with the power of the Holy Spirit. At the Candlestick we thank Jesus that He gave us the gift of the Holy Spirit so we would be a reflection of His great light.

The following piece of furniture was the Table of Shewbread, with four corners, surrounded by a golden crown. It housed the twelve loaves of Shewbread, which were symbolic of the Jewish nation. The Table now represents the four corners of the earth and the Shewbread represents all the people upon God's heart. It is here we enter into our role as intercessors, standing in the gap and repenting for all men.

Next we have the Altar of Incense, which represents the fragrance of *"true worship"*. We thank Jesus for perfecting our prayers and making them a sweet smelling perfume unto the Father. This allows us to go beyond the veil and enter into the presence of God.

At the Ark of the Covenant (Mercy Seat), we worship Father, Son and Holy Spirit and experience perfect communion. This is not only the perfect way to pray and worship the Lord but it will manifest **"The Awesome Power of God!"**

I Peter 2:9
But ye are a chosen generation, a royal priesthood, an holy nation, a peculiar people; that ye should shew forth the praises of him who hath called you out of darkness into his marvellous light:

For years we have read, quoted, and sang these words without understanding their importance. First Peter 2:9 is a powerful scripture that holds the key to the ushering in of the glory of God and the completion of all things He has purposed for mankind. Yes, the key to manifesting the glory is in this scripture, yet even more startling is the fact that the key to this scripture is you! YOU are the key, not the Church as a whole, not your pastor, your prayer group, your mother, father, husband, wife, sister, brother or neighbor—but Y-O-U!

In the Old Testament the high priest would go into the presence of God once a year to make atonement for Israel. Just as it was the duty of the high priest in the Old Testament to enter into the presence of God alone, yet on behalf of all, YOU have also been entrusted with that same power and responsibility.

Revelation 1:5-6 says that the *"Prince of the kings of the earth"* has made us kings and priests unto God. This calling is not optional, if you are a child of God washed by the Blood of Jesus, you have been made a king and a priest. Whether you are a part of the five-fold ministry or a new convert, the first call of God upon your life is to be a king and priest unto Him!

The alarming aspect of this call is that most of us have never been taught the functions or duties of these offices! By the prompting of the Holy Spirit, we began to search the scriptures and receive revelation from Him concerning the requirements of this holy calling. As kings, we are to declare and decree the Word of God, live as royalty and reign with dominion, authority and power. As priests, we are to live holy and become the intercessors God desires to stand in the gap for all men. Furthermore, we are to have communion and fellowship with the Lord and to worship Him in spirit and in truth.

Praying according to the divine order of the Tabernacle of Moses will bless you with each accomplishment. This book will plant your feet firmly on the right path to become what all creation has been waiting for—THE MANIFESTED SONS OF GOD!

The Tabernacle of Moses is also a prophetic timeline for the history of the Church. Each piece of the Tabernacle represents spiritual times and seasons. When the Reformation (1500's) restored the truth that we are saved by faith in Christ alone, the Brazen Altar was reinstated. The Wesley Brothers (1800's) taught the truth of sanctification by the Word, which represents the Laver. The Azusa Street revival in the early 1900's gave us a greater revelation of the Person of Jesus Christ and His anointing, which is represented by the Candlestick. The Charismatic movement in the 1960's, with emphasis on the Holy Spirit and His gifts, restored the Table of Shewbread. We are now in the process of restoring the Altar of Incense, where we become true worshippers unto the Lord and respond to Him as *"Daddy"* our loving Father. True worship allows us to be transported into the Holy of Holies into the very presence of God. This phase is called the *"Saints Movement"*. In this movement Christians will become true worshippers, who worship the Lord in spirit and in truth, and manifest His glory in the earth. Get ready for a complete transformation! As you become one of the greatly sought after worshippers, your life will blossom with the awesome power and presence of God!

In praying according to Pattern, you will notice tremendous growth in all areas of your life. There is also awesome power generated in a corporate setting as Saints unify as one, under the Word of God. The most exciting benefit is that you will be a vital part of God fulfilling His end-time plans and purposes.

We are on the threshold of the most exciting time in human history! Don't you know that you were born to the kingdom for such a time as this! You will not want to miss your part in bringing forth the awesome power of God's glory in these last days. The Word promises that the knowledge of His glory will cover the earth as the waters cover the sea, causing the most awesome revival this world has ever seen! This revival will glorify our Father in the earth; bring about the salvation of lost souls and the perfection of the Saints!

We know that your joy will be full, when you see the rewards of your choice in eternity! So **"Come And Take This Journey With Us!"**

If you have not received Jesus Christ as your personal Lord and Savior, that is where you must begin. Please confess the following prayer out loud:

Dear Heavenly Father,

I come to You in the name of the Lord Jesus Christ. I repent of my sins and I ask for Your forgiveness. I now confess that Jesus is my

Lord and Savior and I believe in my heart that He died for me and was raised from the dead. I ask You Jesus to come into my heart and live Your life through me. At this moment I believe that I am born again by an act of Your love, grace and mercy. Thank You for saving my soul. Amen.

Rom 10:9-10
That if thou shalt confess with thy mouth the Lord Jesus, and shalt believe in thine heart that God hath raised him from the dead, thou shalt be saved. For with the heart man believeth unto righteousness; and with the mouth confession is made unto salvation.

Come And Take This Journey With Me!

I bring repentance and thanksgiving,
Entering in by the *"WAY"*
For the Blood You shed for my sins,
I am so thankful each and every day.
The light of day or natural light
Is available, allowing me to see;
The Blood You shed on Calvary, for the world,
And thank God just for me!

The Blood that speaks of better things
Than that of Abel, even now;
It calls to the world in earnest longings;
"My children, where art thou?"
Then I enter into *"TRUTH"*, Your Word
Having washed and set me apart;
To be illuminated by the Candlestick,
So that I can begin to know Your heart.

The Light of the world, brings the light of the Word,
And I will glorify Your name;
And I know that in this, I am marked for life
And I will never be the same.
There's complete satisfaction as I receive
The "Bread of Life"; Lord I understand the cost;
So I bear the world upon my shoulders and heart,
As I bring intercession for the lost.

As I enter into the veil called *"LIFE"*,
Where the veil of Your flesh was torn;

As I bring true worship in love to You,
To Your life and purpose, I'll conform.
I worship You in the beauty of holiness;
I'll give glory due Your name.
And as I give You glory, honor, and strength,
You'll bring the promises I have claimed.

I no longer need natural light or candlelight
To obtain the promises You have for me;
Because now I'm in Your presence,
And Your goodness and glory, now I see!
Praise God, I have entered into the realm,
Where the God in Christ; becomes Christ in me!
This ageless truth hidden from
the prudent and wise;
That Christ in me; is the hope of glory!

I've partaken of the Heavenly Gift,
I am a carrier of Your presence this day.
With the Word of God in my heart;
To blossom in fruitfulness, is the only way.
As I learn to abide in, walk in; and live in
The overflow of Your glory;
The world will know that I've been with You;
And I will be sure and tell the story!

And I'll invite them all to come with me,
And know what I have been graced to see;
All it takes is the willingness of heart,
To come and take this journey with me!

The Tabernacle
Prayer Pattern Illustration

ARK OF THE COVENANT
Jesus the Carrier
of the Presence of God

7. THE HOLY OF HOLIES - THE PRESENCE OF GOD
For Thine Is The Kingdom, And The Power,
And The Glory, For Ever. A-Men.

THE ALTAR OF INCENSE
Jesus the Apostle
and High Priest

6. PURGE YOUR HEART AND WORSHIP
HIM IN SPIRIT AND IN TRUTH
And Lead Us Not Into Temptation,
But Deliver Us From Evil

THE LAMPSTAND
Jesus the Light
of the World

TABLE OF SHEWBREAD
Jesus the Bread
of the Life

4. THANK GOD FOR THE ANOINTING
OF THE HOLY GHOST
In Earth, As It Is In Heaven

5. STAND IN THE GAP, REPENT AND
INTERCEDE FOR ALL MEN
Give Us This Day Our Daily Bread. And Forgive
Us Our Debts, As We Forgive Our Debtors

BRAZEN LAVER
Jesus the Word
of God made flesh

3. THANK GOD FOR HIS WORD
Thy Will Be Done

BRAZEN ALTAR
Jesus the sinless Lamb
became the Eternal Sacrifice

2. THANK GOD FOR THE BLOOD OF JESUS CHRIST
Thy Kingdom Come

1. REPENT AND ENTER HIS GATES WITH THANKSGIVING
Our Father Which Art In Heaven, Hallowed Be Thy Name

The Tabernacle Prayer

YOUR KING-PRIEST MINISTRY

Revelation 1:5-6 states the Blood of Jesus has made us kings and priests unto God. As kings we are to declare and decree the Word of God. As priests we are to become true worshippers and intercessors praying for the perfection of the Saints and the salvation of lost souls. Therefore, as you pray keep in mind you are a king-priest fulfilling the Word of God. You have been anointed and appointed to stand in the gap and intercede for the world.

This prayer is constructed in the order of the Tabernacle of Moses. It is also in the order of the Lord's Prayer in **Matthew 6:9-13.** Before you begin any prayer you need to repent. **Psalms 66:18** states, that if you regard iniquity in your heart, the Lord will not hear you. Therefore it is appropriate that you take care of your sin by repenting. This prayer is designed to be short and can be read in approximately fifteen minutes. However, you can take your time by praying the Word and then praying in tongues. We recommend that you pray this prayer each morning and/or record it on tape so you can play it and pray along. It is necessary that you fill up your spirit with prayer daily. This Prayer Pattern is unlimited, so feel free to find your own scriptures. Talk to God in your own words; just make sure that you use one or more scriptures for each section. Remember God's Word will not return unto Him void, so use His Word to make your prayers more powerful.

1 *The Gate-Repentance*
FATHER WE REPENT AND CONFESS OUR SINS.

Father, have mercy upon us according to Your loving kindness and tender mercies and blot out our transgressions. Wash us from iniquity and cleanse us from sin. For against You and You only we have sinned **(Ps 51:1-4).** Father in the name of Jesus, we repent for every sin, known, unknown, omitted, and committed. We repent for unforgiveness and we release and forgive all **(Mark 11:25).** We ask You to cleanse us from secret faults and keep us back from presumptuous sins; and let them not have dominion over us: then we shall be upright, and innocent from the great transgression **(Ps 19:12-13).** Father, we thank You that Your Word says in **I John 1:9,** If we confess our sins, You are faithful and just to forgive us, and to cleanse us from all unrighteousness. Create in us a clean heart and renew a right spirit within us and let the words of our mouth and the meditation of our heart be acceptable in Your sight O Lord our strength and Redeemer **(Ps 51:10) -- (Ps 19:14).**

The Gate-Thanksgiving

FATHER WE ENTER YOUR GATES WITH THANKSGIVING.
[Our Father Which Art In Heaven, Hallowed Be Thy Name]

Father we praise You, hallow Your holy name, and thank You for Your love. Lord we praise You for Your mighty acts and we praise You according to Your excellent greatness **(Ps 150:1-2).** O Lord, our Lord how excellent is Your name in all the earth **(Ps 8:1)!** The name of the Lord is a strong tower and the righteous run into it and are safe **(Prov 18:10).** O magnify the Lord with us, and let's exalt His name together **(Ps 34:3).** The Lord's name is to be praised from the rising of the sun to the going down of the same **(Ps 113:3).** Every day we will bless You Lord, and we will praise Your name forever and ever **(Ps 145:2).**

(Continue to bless the Lord and give thanks for all that He has done for you)

- 24 -

2 The Brazen Altar

FATHER, THANK YOU FOR THE BLOOD OF JESUS CHRIST.

[Thy Kingdom Come]

Father, thank You for loving us so much that You gave Your only begotten Son, that whosoever shall believe in Him should not perish but have everlasting life **(John 3:16)**. He was wounded for our transgressions, He was bruised for our iniquities: the chastisement of our peace was upon Him; and with His stripes we are healed **(Isa 53:5)**. Thank You Lord Jesus for blotting out the handwriting of the ordinances that were against us and taking them out of the way by nailing them to Your cross. In the process You defeated and triumphed over every evil power and made a show of them openly **(Col 2:14-15)**. Father God, we thank You for the precious Blood of Jesus that was shed for the remission of all our sins. We plead and apply the Blood of Jesus to every part of our lives and every precious stone in our breastplate. **Gal 3:13** assures us that Christ has redeemed us from every curse over our lives, that we may partake of the blessings of Abraham. Thank You Lord Jesus for redeeming us by Your Blood and making us king-priests unto God to reign on this earth **(Rev 5:9-10)**. Father we thank

You that Your kingdom has come in our lives.

3 *The Brazen Laver*
FATHER THANK YOU FOR YOUR WORD.
[Thy Will Be Done]

Father, we thank You that **John 1:1** says, in the beginning was the Word, and the Word was with God, and the Word was God. **John 1:14** says that the Word was made flesh, and dwelt among us, (and we beheld His glory, the glory of the only begotten of the Father), full of grace and truth. Jesus is the Word made flesh. Your Word is made flesh or manifested in our lives, as we establish Your Word upon this earth. Your Word is health and healing to all of our flesh **(Prov 4:22)**. Your Word is quick and powerful and sharper than any two-edged sword and is able to divide the soul and spirit, the joints and marrow, and discern the thoughts and intents of the heart **(Heb 4:12)**. Your Word is a lamp unto our feet, and a light unto our path **(Ps 119:105)**. We receive the blessings of **Deut 28:1-14**, because we hearken diligently unto Your Word. We thank You Father that we have been sanctified and cleansed with the washing of water by the Word of God **(Eph 5:26)**. Your Word is Your will, therefore let Your will be done in our lives.

4 *The Golden Candlestick*

FATHER THANK YOU FOR THE ANOINTING OF THE HOLY SPIRIT.
[In Earth, As It Is In Heaven]

In **John 8:12** Jesus said, I am the Light of the world and He that follows Me shall not walk in darkness but shall have the light of life. Father thank You for the light of life, which is the anointing. Jesus is the "Light of the world" and He has caused us to be a reflector of that light, which will bring glory to our Heavenly Father **(Matt 5:14-16)**. **Acts 10:38** states, that God anointed Jesus of Nazareth with the Holy Ghost and with power: who went about doing good, and healing all that were oppressed of the devil; for God was with Him. We are also anointed with the Holy Spirit and we are born of God for the purpose of destroying the works of darkness **(I John 3:8)**. Jesus said in **John 14:12,** He that believes on Me, the works that I do he shall do also and greater works than these. Thank You

- 27 -

Lord for the anointing of the Holy Spirit and the gifts of the Spirit to do these greater works. We ask You, Holy Spirit, to flow through us as You purpose with Your gifts, the gift of faith, gifts of healing, working of miracles, word of wisdom, word of knowledge, discerning of spirits, tongues, interpretation of tongues, and prophecy **(I Cor 12:8-10)**. We have the sevenfold anointing; the Spirit of the Lord, the spirit of wisdom and understanding, the spirit of counsel and might, the spirit of knowledge, and of the fear of the Lord **(Isa 11:2)**. Father, correct us, so that nothing will hinder Your power from flowing through us and we can bring forth pure and holy light. Father, we thank You for the Holy Spirit, Who brings forth Your power from heaven. We also thank You for allowing us to share Your light all over this world.

5 *The Table Of Shewbread*

FATHER WE STAND IN THE GAP AND REPENT FOR ALL. THANK YOU THAT JESUS IS THE BREAD OF LIFE AND OUR POWER TO DO BATTLE. WE SPIRITUALLY PARTAKE OF COMMUNION, PUT ON YOUR ARMOR AND INTERCEDE FIRST FOR YOUR PURPOSES AND THEN PRAY OUR OWN

PETITIONS.

[Give Us This Day Our Daily Bread. And Forgive Us Our Debts, As We Forgive Our Debtors]

Father as we come to Your Table as king-priests and intercessors, we stand in the gap for the Jews, the entire Body of Christ, the unsaved, and for the leaders of this world **(Ezek 22:30).** We stand in the gap and repent for we have all sinned, transgressed Your laws, committed iniquity, shed innocent blood, operated in unforgiveness, and have done wickedly in Your sight. **I John 1:9** says, if we confess our sins, You are faithful and just to forgive us. Father forgive and cleanse us with the Blood of Jesus. Father, as we spiritually partake of communion, the broken body and shed Blood of Jesus, we thank You that Jesus is the "Bread of Life". His body and Blood is our nourishment, strength and power to be victorious over all works of the enemy. It is also the "Children's Bread of Deliverance", therefore we are delivered from every foe within and without. We put on the whole of armor of God according to **Eph 6:10-20.** We are strong in the Lord and in the power of His might. The weapons of our warfare are not carnal but they are mighty through God for the pulling down of strongholds **(II Cor 10: 4-5).** You have given us authority to tread upon serpents and scorpions, and over all of the power of the enemy and nothing shall by any means hurt us **(Luke 10:19).** We bind every strong man that is set against us and loose the Angel of the Lord to plunder their house and spoil their goods **(Matt 12:29).** According to **II Tim 4:18,** Father we declare that You will deliver us from every evil work and preserve us for Your heavenly kingdom. We pray that the unsaved will come to know Jesus Christ as Lord and Savior **(Ps 2:8).** We ask for the heathen nations as our inheritance and the uttermost parts of the earth as our possession. We also pray for the fear of God to fall upon every leader all over the world, thereby bringing them to repentance. We declare that Your people will lead a quiet and peaceable life in all godliness and honesty and the gospel of Jesus Christ will continue to spread unhindered all over the world **(I Tim 2:2).** Father we ask that we receive the spirit of wisdom and revelation in the knowledge of You, that the eyes of our understanding are enlightened that we might know the hope of our calling and to know the surpassing fullness of Your love **(Eph 1:17-23 -- 3:14-21).** We pray for the peace of Jerusalem, peace within their walls and prosperity within their palaces and we seek their highest good **(Ps 122:6-9).** We pray that the Body of Christ will come into the unity of faith, unto the knowledge of the Son of God, unto a perfect man, to the measure of the stature of the fullness of Christ **(Eph 4:13).**

(You can now pray your own petitions)

6 *The Altar Of Incense*

FATHER CLEANSE OUR HEARTS AND PERFECT YOUR LOVE AND THE FRUIT OF THE SPIRIT WITHIN US. *[And Lead Us Not Into Temptation, But Deliver Us From Evil]*

Father create in us a clean heart, O God; and renew a right spirit within us **(Ps 51:10).** Perfect Your love in our lives according to **I Cor 13.** We want the fruit of the Spirit to ripen in us **(Gal 5:22-23 - II Peter 1:5-8).** We pray for love, joy, peace, longsuffering, gentleness, goodness, faith, meekness and temperance: balanced with the gifts of the Spirit **(I Cor 12:8-10).** Father God, we bring You worship attitudes of spontaneity, honesty, transparency, brokenness, the sweet fragrance of Jesus, and covenant speech. We ask You to come into our hearts, and let the light of Your countenance purge away all that is not pleasing to You and deliver us from evil **(Ps 4:6).** We bring to You our weaknesses, hurts, wounds, broken dreams and broken hearts. We cast all of our cares upon You for You care for us **(I Peter 5:7)**. **Heb 7:25** says that Jesus is able to deliver us and ever lives to make intercession for us. Jesus is the Apostle and High Priest of our profession and confession **(Heb 3:1)**. We thank You Lord Jesus for perfecting our prayers, worship, and all that concerns us **(Ps 138:8)**. We also ask You to take the coal and cleanse our lips, for life and death are in the power of the tongue **(Prov 18:21)**. Put a guard over our mouths so that we will say only Your words of peace and prosperity over ourselves and others **(Col 4:6)**. Father we thank You that we have a covenant relationship with You. We are blessed of God Most High, the possessor of heaven and earth and blessed be God Most High; that has delivered all of our enemies into our hand **(Gen 14:19-20)**.

7 *The Ark Of The Covenant*

FATHER THANK YOU FOR LETTING US COME INTO YOUR HOLY PRESENCE.
[For Thine Is The Kingdom, And The Power, And The Glory, For Ever. A-Men.]

You have shown us the path of life: in Your presence is fullness of joy; at Your right hand there are pleasures for evermore **(Ps 16:11).** Daddy thank You for the precious Blood of Jesus that is speaking from the Mercy Seat, proclaiming greater things than that of Abel **(Heb 12:24).** We are so grateful Daddy, that when You look at us, You do not see us, but You see Jesus. Daddy God, thank You for making us vessels that are filled with Your presence **(Col 1:27).** Your Laws are written upon our hearts and in our minds **(Heb 8:10).** We speak and declare the truth of Your Word. We have revelation knowledge, and bud, blossom and bring forth fruit in resurrection power. The fruit and the gifts of the Spirit are operating in our lives in perfect balance. We are like the Ark, golden vessels, filled with Your covenant promises and with Your glory **(Isa 60:1-3).** We worship You, Daddy, as the Giver and the Source of all life. We worship You, Holy Spirit, and we thank You for being the lover of our souls, our Comforter and our closest friend. We worship You, Lord Jesus, for You are the King of Glory, the Lord of Hosts, Captain of heaven's armies, and the Lord strong and mighty **(Ps 24:7).** We declare that Jesus is Lord, and His dominion is everlasting. For thine is the kingdom, the power and the glory for ever and ever, Amen.

Then begin to worship the entire Godhead with the fruit of your lips, and with a "new song" in tongues or your understanding (I Cor 14:15). The Lord may also have you read scripture to Him. The Psalms and/or Revelation 5 are always great.

**FOLLOW THE HOLY SPIRIT AND
WE GUARANTEE YOU, YOUR
LIFE WILL NEVER BE
THE SAME!!!**

**WE OVERCOME BY THE BLOOD
OF THE LAMB AND THE WORD
OF OUR TESTIMONY!!!
(Rev 12:11)**

Short Tabernacle Prayer

Father we come to You in the name of Jesus, repenting of all of our sins. We repent for sins known and unknown, sins of word, thought and deed, and also secret faults **(Ps 51:1-4)**. Cleanse us according to **I John 1:9;** Your Word states if we confess our sins, You are faithful and just to forgive us and cleanse us from all unrighteousness. Father we enter Your gates with thanksgiving and Your courts with praise, exalting the name of Jesus which is above every name **(Eph 1:20-21)**. We declare that Jesus is Lord over this day.

Father we thank You that Jesus is the Lamb of God, Who shed His Blood for our sins and complete deliverance **(John 1:29 - John 3:16)**.

Father, we also thank You that Jesus is the Word made flesh **(John 1:14)** and You sent Your Word to heal us and deliver us from our destructions **(Ps 107:20)**. We also thank You for washing us by the water of Your Word so we can come forth as Your bride, holy and pure **(Eph 5:26-27)**.

We exalt You Father for the power and the anointing of the Holy Spirit, making us Your Lampstand **(Matt 5:14-16)**. We reflect Your light and walk in miracles, signs, and wonders.

Father we come to stand in the gap and repent for all mankind. We have all sinned and fallen short of Your glory and we ask for Your forgiveness **(Dan 9:5, 19)**.   As we spiritually receive communion, the broken body and shed Blood of Jesus, we gain full power to war, battle and overcome. We put on the whole armor of God and pray for every precious stone in our breastplate, the Lost, the Leadership, the Body of Christ and the Jewish Nation **(I Tim 2:1-4)**. We declare that the Lord will deliver us from every evil work and preserve us for His heavenly kingdom – to Him be the glory for ever and ever **(II Tim 4:18)**.   We pray for the peace of Jerusalem, peace within their walls, and prosperity within their palaces **(Ps 122:6-9)**.   Father we thank You for the blessing over our lives that You promised us for praying for Israel **(Gen 12:3)**. We thank You that we all come into the unity of faith perfected in Christ **(Eph 4:13)**.

We come to You as true worshippers in the earth, worshipping You in spirit and in truth **(John 4:23-24)**.   We purge our hearts and bring that perfect blend of heart motivations and attitudes **(Gal 5:22-23)**. We exalt Jesus the Apostle and High Priest of the House of God. He makes this prayer and our worship perfect before You and leads us into Your presence **(Heb 3:1)**.

Father we come beyond the Veil into Your presence, worshipping at the Mercy Seat, Your throne of grace **(Heb 4:16).** We worship You Father, Jesus the Lamb of God, and Holy Spirit in the joy of Your presence **(Ps 16:11).** We exalt You, Father, and magnify Your name and the name of Jesus in all the earth. We love You and we thank You for loving us! For thine is the kingdom, the power and the glory forever! Amen **(Matt 6:13).**

Tips On Praying The Pattern

Do not concern yourself with time. God is so great in manifold wisdom that this type of prayer can be completed in one minute, or it can be transformed into an all night vigil. This prayer usually takes about fifteen minutes. You can also alternate praying the steps of the pattern with a prayer partner---or each person in a group, can pray a segment of the Pattern to complete the prayer. You can do it anywhere or at any time. As long as you do it according to Pattern you will experience the manifested presence of God!

Other Suggestions:

- *Record yourself reading the full Prayer Pattern. You will be amazed at hearing how powerful you sound praying the Word of God.*
- *Play your recorded prayer often and pray along with it to get it into your spirit.*
- *Do not quote scripture references in the Prayer Pattern that are within parenthesis.*
- *Utilize the Short Prayer for quick access to God's presence.*
- *We also encourage you to create your own short prayer using the model at the end of*

this chapter. When you become comfortable with praying it, continue to add scriptures to grow your prayer.

- Always bind Psalms 91 to everyone after completing major warfare.
- Last but not least, enhance your prayer even further by using God's Jewish Names. He loves it! Jesus can be referred to as Yeshua (Our Salvation) or Yahshua (Our God is our Salvation). The Holy Spirit can be referred to as the Ruach HaKodesh and God the Father as YHVH or Yahweh!

Model For Creating
Your Own Prayer

1. Repent
*(Father We Repent And Confess
Our Sins)*

_____
_____
_____
_____

Enter His Gates With Thanksgiving
*[Our Father Which Art In Heaven, Hallowed
Be Thy Name]*

_____
_____
_____
_____

2. Thank God For The Blood Of Jesus Christ
[Thy Kingdom Come]

_____
_____
_____
_____

3. Thank God For His Word
[Thy Will Be Done]

_____
_____
_____
_____

4. **Thank God For The Anointing Of The Holy Spirit**
   [In Earth, As It Is In Heaven]

   _____
   _____
   _____
   _____

5. **Stand In The Gap, Repent, And Intercede For The World**
   [Give Us This Day Our Daily Bread. And Forgive Us Our Debts, As We Forgive Our Debtors]

   _____
   _____
   _____
   _____

6. **Purge Your Heart And Worship God In Spirit And In Truth**
   [And Lead Us Not Into Temptation, But Deliver Us From Evil]

   _____
   _____
   _____
   _____

7. **Worship The Father, Son And Holy Spirit**
   [For Thine Is The Kingdom, And The Power, And The Glory, For Ever. A-Men.]

   _____
   _____
   _____
   _____

Pray With Us

It is our desire to see true worshippers cover the earth. If you have been touched by this book and have decided to enter into your holy calling, we would like to know. Please visit our web site and register. We have a global map that we use to mark places where people are praying according to Pattern. We will one day fulfill our destiny to worship God in unity as one man! The Body of Christ praying and worshipping according to Pattern can achieve this. Let's pray the eternal purposes of God according to Ephesians 4:13, *"Till we all come in the unity of the faith, and of the knowledge of the Son of God, unto a perfect man, unto the measure of the stature of the fulness of Christ"*.

Numbers 6:24-26

The LORD bless thee, and keep thee:
The LORD make his face shine upon
thee, and be gracious unto thee: The
LORD lift up his countenance
upon thee, and give
thee peace

From The Heart Of Sandy & C.J.

For more in-depth information and scriptures regarding your royal priesthood and how to pray according to the Pattern order:
"The Awesome Power Of God Praying According To The Pattern"

Visit our web site: www.myholycall.com
Email: prayer@myholycall.com